KEEPING PETS

Guinea Pigs

Tristan Boyer Binns

Heinemann
LIBRARY

www.heinemann.co.uk/library
Visit our website to find out more information about Heinemann Library books.

To order:
 Phone 44 (0) 1865 888066
Send a fax to 44 (0) 1865 314091
Visit the Heinemann bookshop at www.heinemann.co.uk/library to browse our catalogue and order online.

First published in Great Britain by Heinemann Library, Halley Court, Jordan Hill, Oxford OX2 8EJ, part of Harcourt Education.

Heinemann is a registered trademark of Harcourt Education Ltd.

© 2006 Harcourt Education Ltd.
First published in paperback in 2007.
The moral right of the proprietor has been asserted.

Editorial: Andrew Farrow and Stig Vatland
Design: Richard Parker and Q2A Solutions
Picture Research: Maria Joannou and Virginia Stroud-Lewis
Production: Chloe Bloom

Originated by Modern Age Repro
Printed and Bound in China
by South China Printing Company

10 digit ISBN: 0 431 12427 2 (hardback)
13 digit ISBN: 978 0 431 12427 8

10 digit ISBN: 0 431 12454 X (paperback)
13 digit ISBN: 978 0 431 12454 4

10 09 08 07 06
10 9 8 7 6 5 4 3 2 1

British Library Cataloguing in Publication Data
Binns, Tristan Boyer
Guinea pigs. - (Keeping pets)
1.Guinea pigs as pets - Juvenile literature
636.9'3592

A full catalogue record for this book is available from the British Library.

Acknowledgements
The publishers would like to thank the following for permission to reproduce photographs: Alamy Images pp. **5 top** (Bruce Coleman Inc/Jane Burton), **5 bottom** (Juniors Bildarchiv); Corbis pp. **27**, **27**; Ginny Stroud Lewis p. **27**; Harcourt Education Ltd (Tudor Photography) pp. **6 bottom, 6 top, 7, 8, 9 bottom, 10 left, 10 right, 11, 12, 14, 15, 16, 17 bottom, 18, 19 left, 19 right, 20 bottom, 20 top, 21, 22 bottom, 22 top, 23 bottom, 23 middle, 23 top, 24, 26, 27, 28, 30, 32 bottom, 32 middle, 32 top, 34, 35 bottom, 35 top, 36, 37 bottom, 37 top, 38, 41 bottom, 41 top, 42, 43, 45 bottom, 45 middle, 45 top**; Nature Picture Library p. **4**; RSPCA Photo Library pp. **40** (Angela Hampton), **9 top** (E A Janes); Tammy Raabe Rao p. **39**.

Cover photograph reproduced with permission of Getty Images (Iconica/G K and Vikki Hart).

Every effort has been made to contact copyright holders of any material reproduced in this book. Any omissions will be rectified in subsequent printings if notice is given to the publishers.

The paper used to print this book comes from sustainable resources.

Contents

Any words appearing in the text in bold, **like this**, are explained in the glossary.

What is a guinea pig?

Some people think guinea pigs are smelly or boring. They are wrong! Guinea pigs are great pets. They are friendly, with their own **personalities** and habits. They do not smell if they are looked after properly. Many families become life-long fans after getting their first pet guinea pigs.

From the wild

Guinea pigs are **mammals**. They give birth to live babies and feed them milk. Scientists also **classify** them as **rodents**. Wild guinea pigs are also known as cavies.

Guinea pigs are wild animals in South America. People started keeping them for food, and some people still do. About five hundred years ago, people started bringing them to Europe to keep as pets. They might be called "guinea" pigs because sailors brought them back to England through the country of Guinea, and people thought they were from there. They are called "pigs" because of the grunting and squeaking noises that they make. Later, settlers took guinea pigs to America and Australia.

This wild guinea pig lives in the grasslands in Peru.

Guinea pigs are happiest in groups, both in the wild and as pets.

Wild guinea pigs

Wild guinea pigs are thinner, smaller, and much more **alert** than pet ones. You will only find pet guinea pigs for sale in the US, Australia, and Britain. They must be well cared for, and would not survive in the wild.

Need to know

- Having a pet is a big responsibility. Your family should make the decision to get a pet together.
- An adult needs to come with you to the pet shop whenever you buy an animal.
- Most countries have laws protecting animals. It is your responsibility to make sure your guinea pigs are healthy and well cared for.

Guinea pigs have a lot of babies and look after them well.

5

Guinea pig facts

The best way to understand guinea pigs is to learn how they live in the wild. In the wild, guinea pigs live in groups. They spend most of their time eating tough grass. When they see, hear, or smell a threat, they quickly run and hide.

Guinea pigs are about the size of a house brick. They are very low to the ground. Four feet with sharp claws help them to run quickly. Their bodies are shaped well to burrow quickly as they hide. They do not have tails and their small ears are soft and bendy.

Guinea pigs are just the right size for a child. They are easy to care for, usually healthy, and very friendly.

Having somewhere to run and hide makes a guinea pig feel secure.

Senses

Guinea pigs can hear very well – much better than people. Most have a very good sense of smell, too. They can see motion very well. They can even see over the tops of their heads. This helps them to see big birds that might want to eat them in the wild.

Always chewing

Just like wild guinea pigs, pet guinea pigs spend most of their time chewing. Food, hay, grass, wood, cardboard – just about anything they can get their teeth into! Their teeth have no roots, and they never stop growing. If a guinea pig did not keep chewing, its teeth would grow out of its mouth and become a serious problem very quickly. Guinea pigs only eat plants.

Guinea pigs never stop chewing!

Did you know?

- Guinea pigs live for 5-7 years.
- Males are called **boars** and females are called **sows**.
- Babies are born in **litters** of 2-6 babies.
- Babies weigh 57-85 g (2-3 oz) at birth.
- Adults weigh 860-1180 g (30-42 oz).

Mothers and babies

Female guinea pigs should have their first **litter** at about five months old. They have about three babies in each litter. Owners should separate their boy and girl guinea pigs carefully, since they can mate and have babies. Guinea pigs can have up to five litters a year – that is a lot of babies to find homes for! Babies are born **alert**. Their eyes are open, and they have hair. At first, they need their mother's milk and protection. By about six weeks, they can survive on their own, eating solid food.

What kind?

A guinea pig's hair is called its coat. Coats can be short, rough, or long. Long coats are the hardest to care for. The hair can get tangled and knotted very easily. Pure-bred guinea pigs come in many varieties. Mixed breed guinea pigs are generally the healthiest. For a pet, a mixed breed is probably best. If you want to take your guinea pigs to shows where they are judged and can win prizes, you may want to have pure-breds.

This is a Standard Self guinea pig. It has short hair and is the same colour all over.

There are clubs for people who like guinea pigs. They are good places to learn more, and talk with other people who know about guinea pigs. You may even find friends through a local guinea pig club to look after your pets when you go on holiday.

This is a Peruvian (Sheltie) guinea pig. With hair this long, its owner has to brush it every day to keep it healthy.

These are Abyssinian guinea pigs. They have longer hair that whirls out in **rosettes**.

Top tips

Guinea pigs make many different noises.
- They can purr when they feel happy.
- They growl if they feel threatened.
- They make many different squeaks – to say hello, and when they are alarmed or annoyed.
- They can whine or moan when they want to be left alone.

Are guinea pigs for you?

Many guinea pig owners think of their pets as part of the family. They talk about how their pets are friendly and happy to see them. Each guinea pig has a different **personality**, so they really feel like they get to know their pets well. They have fun together.

But owning any pet has good and bad sides. On the next page are some of the good and not-so-good points about owning guinea pigs.

Would you do all the things on the list on page 11, even when you are tired or in a hurry? If the answer is yes, you may be ready to get some pet guinea pigs!

Guinea pigs need play time daily – luckily this is great fun!

Guinea pig cages need attention every day.

Guinea pig good points

- Guinea pigs are intelligent. They get to know you quickly.
- Each guinea pig has its own personality. They have a lot of character and become good friends.
- Guinea pigs are not expensive to buy or feed.
- Guinea pigs learn your routine and are usually ready to play when you are.
- Guinea pigs are quiet, and they do not smell when kept properly.
- Guinea pigs can live for quite a long time. Most pet guinea pigs live for at least five years.

Guinea pig not-so-good points

- Guinea pigs do not like to live alone. You need to have at least two.
- Guinea pigs need enough space to stay happy. Plan to have at least 45 x 65 cm (18 x 25 in) of floor space for each animal.
- You need to have time to feed them, change the water, and clean the cage every day.
- Guinea pigs need play time and exercise outside their cages every day.
- You need to check they are healthy every day, and take them to the vet if they are sick.
- If your guinea pigs live outside, you must bring them in to shelter in hot, cold, wet, or windy weather.
- You need to keep male and female guinea pigs apart, or you may have a lot of unwanted babies.

Choosing your guinea pigs

Now that you have decided to keep guinea pigs as pets, you will want to find healthy ones. Unless one guinea pig spends almost all of its time with human beings, it will get too lonely. You should have two or more so they stay happy.

You can find guinea pigs at good pet shops, animal **shelters**, and **breeders**. A good shelter or breeder can tell you whether the animals are male or female, and guarantee that they are healthy. Pet shop staff may not know as much about guinea pigs, so they might sell you a pregnant **sow** or get the sex wrong. This means you could have guinea pig babies you are not ready for. It is always a good idea to get an expert to double-check the sex. Your expert can show you how to check the animals are healthy.

Many pet shops sell guinea pigs.

Babies or adults?

You can get babies or adults. Both have advantages. Babies are fun to watch as they grow. As you spend time together, they will get to know and trust you. Often adults are pets other people could not keep any more. They may need time to get to know and trust you. If you do get adults, you can feel good about saving them and giving them good homes. It can be very rewarding when they do become your friends.

Specialist breeders may have different types of guinea pig for sale. They will be able to give you more information.

What to look for

- Check the coat by running your fingers through it backwards. The hair should feel silky and strong.
- Look for bald patches and rough or broken skin underneath the coat.
- Check teeth are not broken or growing at odd angles.
- The nose should be dry.
- The eyes should be bright and clear.
- The guinea pig should move quickly and well.

A healthy guinea pig

A healthy baby guinea pig should try to run away and hide when it sees you. This shows it has good **instincts** and a strong body. It will easily learn to know and trust you when you bring it home. An adult should be fairly friendly. Sometimes guinea pigs from an animal **shelter** are not very friendly and might be scared of you. An animal that has been badly treated may need an expert to help it recover and may not be a good first pet.

Guinea pigs always like to have friends to live with.

Top tip

If you get a new baby guinea pig and want it to live with adults, you need to make sure it has somewhere safe to hide while they get to know each other. Give the baby a piece of plastic pipe or a small sturdy house with openings that are too narrow for the adults to fit through. Make sure it has food and water while it is getting used to its new home.

Boars and sows

An expert can tell if a guinea pig is a **boar** or a **sow** from about six weeks old. If you only want two guinea pigs, you can get two boars to live together. More than two boars might fight each other. If you want more than two guinea pigs, then you can keep any number of sows together. If it is possible, get brothers or sisters from the same **litter** because they are already used to each other. To make sure your guinea pigs do not breed, even if someone makes a mistake about their sex, you can get them **neutered**. Talk to your vet about this.

Guinea pigs and rabbits

Guinea pigs are sometimes kept with rabbits. This is not a good idea. The rabbits are usually bigger, and can kick the guinea pigs and really hurt them. Also, guinea pigs and rabbits need different food. Guinea pig food can make rabbits sick. This is because guinea pigs need **vitamin C** in their food to keep healthy, but rabbits do not. Rabbits make vitamin C in their bodies. If they eat too much in their food as well, they will get sick.

When you put a baby in with adults, give it somewhere to escape to so it feels secure.

What do I need?

You need to decide where to keep your guinea pigs. In the wild they live in a warm, fairly dry **environment**. If you live somewhere that is quite warm all year round, you might be able to keep them outside. Their home can be moved into deep shade in the hottest part of the year, and into a shed, porch, or inside your house during the coldest and wettest part of the year. Never keep a guinea pig or any other caged animals in a garage where engines are run! The exhaust fumes could kill them.

Most outdoor guinea pig hutches look like this. It is easy to get inside for cleaning and to get your pets out.

A good hutch

If you decide to keep your pets outside, you need a hutch that is raised off the ground. The hutch can be raised on legs, or secured to a wall or fence. Cats, foxes, and other wild animals will be interested in your pets. Even if the animals cannot get into the hutch, the guinea pigs will be frightened and will get stressed. By raising the hutch, you stop other animals looking inside and threatening your pets.

A good outdoor hutch is made from wood with mesh sides. It needs a sturdy, felted, waterproof roof. There should be a section that is totally enclosed with a door opening into the rest of the hutch. This is a place for the guinea pigs to go when they need somewhere to shelter from **predators** and bad weather, or just to sleep. The hutch should be big enough to give your pets enough space, but small enough to move easily.

Safety tip

It is very important that the base of your cage is smooth. Wire mesh floors can hurt the soft bottoms of guinea pigs' feet. Plastic exercise balls and wire exercise wheels designed for other small pets are not a good idea for guinea pigs. They can hurt their backs and feet in them.

Make sure a store bought cage like this one is big enough for your guinea pigs.

Top tip

Each guinea pig needs at least 3,000 square centimetres (3.2 square feet) of floor space. The more space they have, the more active and happy they will be.

17

Staying inside

Wherever you live, it may be easiest to keep your pets inside. They want to see people around them, so they are happiest in busy parts of the house. They need to be protected from direct sun, radiators, and draughts. If you have cats or dogs, make sure the cage is well off the ground, so the guinea pigs are not bothered by your other pets.

A good indoor cage should have a waterproof base. Most you buy at pet stores have smooth plastic bottoms. Sides made from clear plastic or wire mesh clip onto the base. They can easily be taken off to clean the whole cage out. Some have open tops and others are enclosed all the way around.

It is very important that enough air flows through your pets' cage. A glass **aquarium** makes a bad guinea pig home because the air cannot move around.

The top bedding should always be fresh hay. Underneath you can use newspaper or special wood shavings. Many people use shredded paper or paper pellets, which stop bad smells underneath.

Bedding

Your guinea pigs will use the bedding in their home as a toilet as well. There are many options for bedding. Most people agree that a layer of newspaper topped with fresh hay is the best. The animals eat the hay and burrow through it, making nests and hiding spots. Their **urine** and droppings fall through to the newspaper, making it easier to clean out. You can also use recycled paper pellets or special wood shavings under hay as bedding. Never use straw or cedar shavings because these can hurt your pets.

Food and drink

Your pets will need a water bottle. This should be hung on the outside of the cage. It should have a metal spout with a ball at the end where the water comes out. They also need a food bowl. To stop it tipping over, choose a heavy bowl with a wide base. Some bowls have a fairly narrow top opening to stop guinea pigs sitting in them.

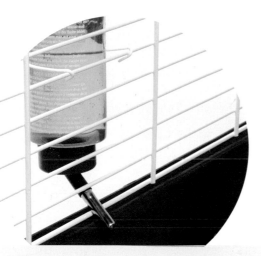

Even a good water bottle will not stop some guinea pigs causing a flood – check for wet areas around the bottle!

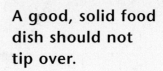

A good, solid food dish should not tip over.

Playtime

Guinea pigs like to play and explore. Give them tunnels, platforms, and hiding houses, and they will be very happy. You can use plumbers' plastic pipes for tunnels. Shoeboxes with holes cut in the sides make good temporary houses. Longer lasting ones need to be made from wood. Ramps and platforms need to have safe edges, not too far off the ground. A side rail is a good idea if possible. Guinea pigs can be hurt badly if they fall from any height. Bricks make great dividers and platforms. Their rough surface helps keep claws trim as well.

If you have a lot of guinea pigs outdoors, you could keep them in a high-rise hutch like this.

Arks like this one let your pets graze safely on your lawn.

Whatever you use in your guinea pigs' home, make sure it will not poison them if chewed. They chew on nearly everything, so watch out for inks, dyes, treated wood, and thin plastic especially.

Guinea pigs need time out of their cage for exercise. You can choose an area of your home and make it safe for them to run free in. You can also use a special bottomless cage made from wood and wire mesh to let them safely graze on your lawn outside. If you do, make sure no chemicals are used on your grass. Garden sprays and lawn treatments can make guinea pigs sick.

This is an ideal guinea-pig-proof area. Check very carefully for wires because they love to chew through them.

Top tips

For indoor exercise, choose a part of your house without any wires near the ground.

- Ask an adult to help with any power or telephone wires that need to be moved.
- Put a towel over any carpeting.
- Be prepared to clean up any **urine** and droppings!
- Make a shelter from a cardboard box.
- Fence off anywhere you do not want your pets to reach.

Now you can sit back and enjoy watching them explore.

Caring for your guinea pigs

It is your responsibility to keep your pets healthy by looking after them properly. You need to look after their home in order to keep their bodies healthy. The best way to do this is to replace the hay bedding every day. They will then have clean hay to eat and snuggle down in. Once a day, also scrub out the water bottle and spout and fill with fresh water.

Cleaning the cage

Once a week, clean out the cage thoroughly. These pictures show you how.

First, get everything you need. Put new hay, new bedding, disinfectant spray, and a dustpan and brush within reach. Put the guinea pigs somewhere safe.

Next, clean out the old bedding. Roll up the newspaper with the hay inside it. Sweep out any shavings or pellets. Put everything into a bin liner.

Then spray the cage with disinfectant specially made to clean animal cages. Wait for it to dry.

Line the cage with an under layer of newspaper, pellets, or shavings. Put a good layer of soft, fresh hay on top.

Put the cleaned water bottle and food dish back where they belong. Put the toys and hiding houses back in too. Finally, put your pets back in their fresh clean home.

What to eat?

Guinea pigs need to eat a variety of foods. They should always have hay. Hay is their main bulk food. It keeps them filled up and also keeps their teeth the right length.

If you have a lawn that is not treated with chemicals, your guinea pigs will love eating the fresh grass. If you can, put your pets out to eat grass every day. Never give them grass clippings. They may have bits of poisonous plants in them that are too small for your pets to avoid.

Guinea pigs also need fruit and vegetables. They are like people in that they do not make **vitamin C** in their bodies. They need to eat enough vitamin C each day to stay healthy. The best sources of vitamin C and other important **nutrients** are fresh vegetables and fruit. You can give a mixture of a few different ones each day.

Since these also have a lot of water in them, guinea pigs get a good deal of their water each day by eating fresh foods. Once or twice a day, feed fresh food. Take any uneaten leftovers out after a couple of hours so they do not rot.

Guinea pigs need fresh fruit and vegetables, hay, and dry food every day to stay healthy.

Dry food

Guinea pigs also need dry food, or pellets. These are bought from the pet shop. Do not use dry food made for rabbits or other small animals. It will not have the right mix for your pets. Make sure the dry food you choose does not have nuts or seeds in it. Guinea pigs can choke on the shells.

Experts disagree on how often to feed guinea pigs dry food. Some say once or twice a day and remove leftovers after an hour or so. This stops the animals from overeating and getting fat. Others say to keep the dry food bowl topped up. You can try both methods and decide which works best for your pets.

Guinea pigs can eat:

Fruit

apples	melon
bananas	oranges
broccoli	pears
grapes	raspberries
kiwi fruit	watermelon

Vegetables

beetroot	mustard greens
brussels sprouts	parsley
cabbage	peppers
carrots and their top greens	spinach
cauliflower leaves	sweetcorn
celery cut into small pieces	tomatoes
cucumber	turnips
dandelion greens	swedes
lettuce	

Watch out!

Whatever kind of fresh and dry food you choose, always start by trying small quantities of it. Guinea pigs will avoid most things that can poison them, but they can also be choosy about food that is good for them. Some will love a certain food, such as grapes, and others will not go near it. This is true for dry food as well. Before you buy a large bag, try a sample to make sure your pets will eat it!

Guinea pigs can get diarrhoea from eating too much spinach or new spring grass. Only give them a little at a time. If they do get diarrhoea, stop giving them grass or spinach until they recover.

Keeping neat and clean

Guinea pigs can get skin **infections**. You can keep them away or at least spot them early by keeping your pets clean. Check them over with your fingers every day. Always wash your hands when you finish playing with your pets.

Long-haired and rough-coated guinea pigs need to be brushed every day. You will need a special soft brush and metal comb for your pets. Be very gentle and patient. Hold the hair close to the skin in one hand and hold the brush in the other. That way as you tug on the hair you do not tug on the skin as well. Start by brushing the underside of the coat. Then comb the top layer over it. Be very careful around the face and rump.

Make sure you do not tug on the guinea pig's skin as you brush or you may get bitten!

Bathing

Guinea pigs should be bathed about every three months or if they get very dirty. You can get special small animal shampoo from the pet shop or your vet. You will need two jugs of warm water and a sink or basin to use.

First put the guinea pig in the sink and pour enough warm water over her to dampen her coat. Then rub in the shampoo until it is well lathered. Be careful of the eyes and ears. Rinse with warm water from the jug until all the lather is gone. Dry the guinea pig with a towel. Keep her somewhere warm and draught-free until she is completely dry.

daffodils

buttercups

foxglove

Poison!

Some plants are poisonous to guinea pigs. Mostly plants that grow from bulbs, such as daffodils, and evergreens are poisonous. Guinea pigs will usually not eat more than a small bit of something that is bad for them. It will taste awful so they will avoid it. But it is best to check your lawn and garden before you put your guinea pig out to graze. Common plants to avoid include:

- Box hedge
- Buttercups
- Deadly nightshade
- Foxglove
- Lily-of-the-valley
- Morning glory
- Rhubarb

Check every day

As well as checking your pets' coats and skins every day, have a general look at them all. Any who are not as active, friendly, or loud as usual need a closer look. So do any that are not as eager for their food or refuse their favourite treats. Pick them up and check over the coat and skin. If they seem normal, have a look in the ears. A lot of wax means it is time for a gentle clean. Runny eyes or nose could mean the animal is ill. Teeth growing at odd angles can make eating impossible. **Sores** around the mouth can mean **infections**. The feet are soft and can get bruised, so make sure they are not sore. If you find nothing obviously wrong but your pet is clearly unhappy, you should talk to your vet.

It is very important to check your pets all over every day to make sure they are well.

Going away

When you are going on holiday or will not be around to care for your pets, it is your responsibility to find another carer. Someone may be happy to stop in twice a day to look after your pets. Guinea pigs will be fine left overnight as long as someone is there to feed them in the evening and again the next morning. You may be able to find someone who will take their cage into their own home if you are going to be away for a long time.

Remember that guinea pigs feel **stress** easily. Changes to their routines and homes worry them. Do your best to make changes slowly. If your carer cannot match your regular schedule, try to slowly change your timings before you go away to match what the carer can do. You can move the time of a feeding by 15 minutes each time until you reach the new time without stressing your pets.

Make sure that you leave plenty of food and bedding for your pets. Show your carer how you feed, check over, brush, clean, and play with your pets. They can then match what you do as closely as possible.

Top tip

- Some guinea pigs cannot eat apples. The acid in the apple juice gives them mouth sores that can make them ill.
- If your pets get scabs around their lips and have been eating apples, stop feeding them apples.
- If they do not get better, talk to your vet.

Handling your guinea pigs

When you get your first guinea pigs, spend time watching how they behave. This is the best way to learn what makes them happy, what puzzles them, and what worries or frightens them. Because they have many **predators** in the wild, they are usually very **alert**. Sudden movements, flashes of light, loud noises, and new smells can make them scared. They may huddle to the ground, run for cover, and screech to warn others. Making sure your pets have hiding boxes or pipes will help them feel safe if they get frightened.

Guinea pigs and other pets

Most caged small animals and guinea pigs can get used to each other's company if they are kept nearby. It is a bit different with large animals such as cats and dogs. If you have a cat or a dog, it thinks of your home as its **territory**. Bringing a new pet into its territory can make it feel threatened.

Short sessions let your pets get used to each other slowly with neither feeling threatened.

Introducing your pets

Start by showing your cat or dog how much you love him. Play with him and make a fuss over him. Then have an adult hold your cat or dog on a short leash while you hold the new guinea pig on your lap. Let the two sniff each other. Always hold your guinea pig firmly but gently and keep the cat or dog firmly under control as well. Never leave them alone together unless the guinea pigs are safe in their cage.

Fight!

Guinea pigs do not fight very often. They may look like they are about to fight, but they are usually just going through a routine that seems to help them get to know each other. They will sniff each other's front and back ends. Then they will growl and start pawing with their back feet. Next their heads will sway from side to side. They will raise their heads up so their teeth are shown off. Usually they stop at this point, when one gives up. Sometimes they will start to chatter their teeth. This means they really are about to fight. Throw a towel over them to stop the fight, and then separate them.

Top tip

Remember you are new to your pets too. Give them time to get used to you. Move slowly and carefully. Let them smell your hand before you try to pick one up. Guinea pigs hardly ever bite, so unless you pull their hair or really worry them, you will be safe.

Picking up a guinea pig

Many guinea pigs will run into a corner and turn their rumps towards you when you reach in to get them. It does not matter whether you pick one up with its head or its rump facing you. Reach in and slip a hand underneath the animal's body.

Place your other hand on top. Use a secure grip but do not squash the animal. Lift it gently and confidently. Move it in to your body for extra security.

Do not walk around holding your guinea pig. Sit down and put it on your lap. Keep your hands nearby, resting gently on its back or stroking it smoothly.

Becoming friends

Watch your guinea pig for signs of restlessness. This can mean she has had enough time with you and would like to go back home. Do not push her too far too soon. Listen to what she is trying to tell you and you will become friends more quickly. When you put your pet back into her cage, either put her in rump first or cup your hand over her face. This will stop her leaping out of your grasp too soon. Always wash your hands when you are finished playing with your pets.

When you and your pets are good friends, you may be able to play more together. Some love having their belly fur rubbed. Others like being stroked under the chin. They may talk to you with purrs, whistles, and coos. They may nuzzle into your neck and want to look into your eyes.

Special care

If you have a pregnant guinea pig, you will need to use extra care when you lift her. Make sure your hand is underneath her whole belly and place your hand on top with care. You need to hold her gently but support all of her securely. Lift pregnant guinea pigs as little as possible.

Top tip

Be very careful when lifting and carrying your pets! Guinea pigs do not leap or bound. Their natural place is close to the ground. If one is dropped or falls from any height, he can be very badly hurt. Sometimes he will not be able to move his legs or feet. At worst he can break his back and die.

Around the house

Guinea pigs love to run around the house if they are allowed. Make sure the whole family is happy with this idea first. Then decide where they will be allowed to go and close off other areas. Guinea pigs drop pellets a great deal, and you will need to be able to get to them to clean them up. They also **urinate**, but less often and in small amounts. Think about the floor coverings and how you will clean the **urine** up, too.

Next, look around for anything that might hurt your pets or that your pets might damage. Poisonous plants, power cables, and telephone wires all need to be moved up out of reach or covered over with a solid, fixed cover. Ask an adult to do this work. Remember that guinea pigs chew anything they can get their teeth on. They will chew through wires and eat into books, magazines, and papers. Move your homework!

It can be great fun to play in a safe area together.

Feeling safe

Think about how to help your pets feel safe. Let them have a safe, dark, enclosed place to run to if they feel worried. Give them a cardboard box on its side or one upside down with a door cut out of it.

Finally, double check that no one has let any other pets into the area, or left a door to the outside open. Keep an eye on your pets while they are out. If they spend a long time out of their cages, make sure they have water bottles within reach. Make sure they are safely back in their home in time for meals and at night.

These two are really good friends now!

Top tip

If you need to take your guinea pigs somewhere, you will need a travelling box.

- Smaller is better than bigger. Too much room to slide around in may make your pets feel **stress**.
- Plenty of air holes are important.
- A strong handle and safe catches will make carrying much easier.
- Put something to absorb urine in the bottom of the box.

When you travel with your guinea pigs, make sure they are safe in a special pet carrier.

Some health problems

At some point, your guinea pigs will need to see a vet. Before you bring any guinea pigs home, find a vet who is able to treat them. Ask people at local guinea pig clubs, other guinea pig owners, and the people you get your pets from for their ideas, too. Make sure you know the opening hours, emergency numbers, and directions to your vet's surgery. It will be much easier to deal with a sick pet if you already know who to call and where to go.

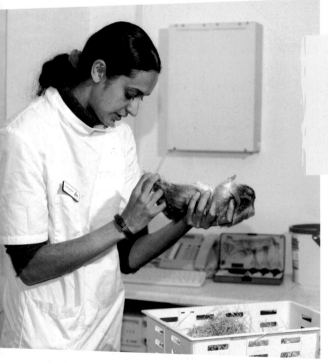

Find a vet who knows a lot about guinea pigs and do not be afraid to ask questions.

Common problems

Guinea pigs are usually very healthy animals. Tell an adult if you think something is wrong with your guinea pig. Here are some of the things that can go wrong.

Eyes

If a guinea pig gets a bit of hay or some other small particle in his eye, it can get irritated. The eye may run with tears or look milky. See if you can find the object that is causing the irritation, or a scratch on the eye itself. Get the object out gently, then wash the eye out with **saline solution**. If it gets red and looks sore or does not start to look normal in a few days, take your guinea pig to the vet.

Mouth

When a guinea pig is not chewing enough, or chews unevenly, her teeth can grow at odd angles. They may grow too long for the animal to eat at all. The vet will need to trim them back correctly. Guinea pigs can get **fungal** mouth **sores,** too. These are treated with an anti-fungal gel.

A healthy foot should look like this.

Feet

Overgrown claws can cause a guinea pig pain, so keep them trimmed properly. Bumblefoot is a painful swelling of the bottom of the foot. Sometimes it gets sores on it as well. It is treated with anti-fungal medicine from your vet.

Guinea pigs' claws need to be trimmed regularly. If they get too long, they can split or hurt. Ask an adult or vet to do this. Be careful not to cut too close to the foot.

Should I call the vet?

First, ask an adult to call the vet when you think something is wrong. If the vet thinks you can treat it yourself, then follow the advice he or she gives. As you get older and more experienced, you will learn more about how to treat sick animals. You can also learn from books, the Internet, and friends.

Digestion

Sometimes guinea pigs get dramatic hiccups. They may look like they are about to vomit, but guinea pigs cannot **vomit**. Hiccups usually stop on their own after a while. If something along the **digestive system** blocks the way, guinea pigs can get bloat. The stomach swells up and the animal does not want to eat or drink. If you think your pet has bloat, see your vet at once.

Guinea pigs also get diarrhoea, especially if they have just started eating fresh fruit and vegetables or new green spring grass. Most of the time there is no need to worry, but sometimes it can be the **symptom** of a bigger problem. Stop feeding your guinea pigs all greens. See your vet if the diarrhoea does not stop soon.

A healthy guinea pig has droppings like these.

Skin and hair

Scaly or scabby patches on a guinea pig's skin can be a sign of a **fungal infection**. Bald patches and thinning hair can mean **parasites**. Both need medicine from the vet. Guinea pigs can get cysts, which are like spots, on their skin. They may also grow lumps under the skin. Cysts need to be opened up by a vet so they do not get too big. Any lumps or bumps should be checked by a vet to make sure they are not harmful.

Sometimes guinea pigs chew their own or another guinea pig's hair. This is called "barbering". It may be caused by boredom, but no one is really sure why they do it. They usually stop after a while. If they seem to be scratching or pulling their hair, check for skin **infections**.

Poison

If your guinea pig eats a poisonous plant by mistake, he will start to shake. He will go weak and not be able to keep his head lifted up. If he breathes or eats a poisonous chemical, he may not be able to breathe properly or have bad diarrhoea. If you think your pet has been poisoned, take him to the vet as quickly as possible.

When they get old, the lenses in some guinea pigs' eyes get cloudy. These are called cataracts and make it harder for the animal to see.

Zoonoses

Zoonoses are diseases that pass between animals and humans. The only ones that guinea pigs get are fungal skin infections. If your pet has a fungal skin infection, wash your hands very carefully after touching him. It is best that an adult treats the guinea pig while he is infected.

Parasites

Guinea pigs can get **parasites** such as head lice or nits. They should be treated with special shampoo. Parasites such as **worms** can also get into their **digestive systems** and make them sick. The vet can give you a wormer to use.

Some guinea pigs can get flystrike, which can kill them. This happens when blowflies lay their eggs in dirty or very long hair. When the eggs hatch, the **larvae** grow very quickly. Old and long-haired guinea pigs are most at risk. Brushing and cleaning your animals well should keep them safe. If you put your guinea pigs outside in summer, you can wipe their rear ends with citronella or lavender essential oil to keep the blowflies away.

These bald patches could be a sign of parasites.

First Aid

If your guinea pig does not have a shaded place to go to escape the sunlight and heat, she may get heat exhaustion. She can pant, have a fast heartbeat, and collapse. She will also be very hot. Take her somewhere shaded and cool, then wrap her in a towel soaked in cold water. When your pet starts to move, take the towel off. Keep her cool but do not let her get chilled. When she starts to act more normally, give her a little water using a syringe. Over time, let her have more water. Within a day she should be back to normal.

If your guinea pig has a small bite wound, treat it like you would a cut on a person. Wash it out with salty water. Put a bit of lavender oil or safe antiseptic cream on it. If it gets red or swollen, or **pus** starts to come out of it, see your vet.

If you have to give a guinea pig medicine, you will probably use a dropper or syringe in the corner of her mouth. An adult should do this for you.

Top tip

Guinea pigs can be very hard to hold if you need to treat or examine them. The best way to keep a guinea pig still is to wrap her in a towel. Tuck the front legs in first, then wrap the rest of the body snugly but not tightly. Leave the head out. Being wrapped up usually makes a guinea pig relax and feel safe. Keep calm and talk to your pet in soft tones to help her stay relaxed.

A well-wrapped guinea pig should look safe and relaxed.

Growing old

As guinea pigs grow older, they want to sleep more and play less. They may feel the cold more, so make sure their home does not get too cool and that they have plenty of hay to snuggle in. They will still be your friends, and want to be stroked and held. They may not want to run around as much as before or be able to move as freely. Taking care of older guinea pigs can be very rewarding. You can help them feel comfortable after they have given you many happy times.

This guinea pig is six years old, but is still healthy and happy. Guinea pigs can live for seven years.

Peaceful endings

Most older guinea pigs stay healthy and fairly active until they die peacefully in their sleep. Some older guinea pigs get diseases such as cataracts or fatty eye, when the eyelids bulge out. These do not cause the animal any pain. Others may get many **infections** and feel bad. Your vet might say that your pet's life is becoming miserable. You might want to talk about putting your guinea pig to sleep. To do this, the vet gives him an injection that makes him sleepy. His heart stops, then he dies. He does not feel any pain. He just feels very sleepy and closes his eyes gently.

It can help to have a burial place for your pet. You could plant flowers on it to mark it as special.

Saying goodbye

It is hard to say goodbye to a pet you have loved. You may have spent many years as friends, or only a short time. When a pet dies, it is normal for both children and adults to feel sad. You may want to cry for a while. After a time, the pain will pass and you will be left with happy memories of your pet. You may have other guinea pigs already, or you may be ready to think about getting more to look after and enjoy.

Keeping a record

Even before you get your guinea pigs, you can start a scrapbook. Get a big one, and start adding information about how to care for guinea pigs, pictures of breeds you like, and interesting cage set-ups.

Useful information

When you bring your pets home, you can add information about them. It is fun to look back on how they reacted to their new home, what you did to get used to each other, and how you set up their cage. Take pictures of them in their new home. Add pictures of you with your new pets. Record how much they weighed and what they like to eat.

You can write down when they do funny things, or even when they do naughty things. You can write down their routine and also what they think of new things. How do they react to new guinea pigs? Do they like your dog?

As you read and learn about caring for guinea pigs, update the information in your scrapbook. If your pets get sick, what helps them get better?

Clubs and shows

If you join any clubs or societies you can keep that information in your scrapbook, too. Some hold shows that you can go along to. If your pets win any ribbons, you can put them in the scrapbook.

Photos are a great way to remember the good times you have with your pets.

Make sure you add captions and dates to your scrapbook photos so you can remember when you took them!

Try to take some nice photos of your guinea pigs to put in your scrapbook.

Glossary

alert   when an animal is wide awake and interested in the place it is in

aquarium   tank made from see-through glass or plastic with an open top

boar   a male guinea pig

breeder   someone who breeds animals

classify   put in a group with

digestive system   part of the body where food is turned into nutrients and waste is produced

environment   the kind of place something lives in, with its plants, animals, weather, temperature, and landscape

fungal   caused by a fungus, which is a growth of very tiny things that live on other living beings

infections   when an illness takes over a normally healthy part of the body

instincts   things animals do without thinking about them

larvae   wormlike young of many insects

litter   a group of babies born at the same time to the same parents

mammals   animals with fur or hair on their bodies that feed their babies with milk

neutered   having an operation that stops an animal having babies

nutrients   the things in food that animals and plants need to keep healthy

parasites   small creatures, such as worms or mites, that live on or in another creature

personality   the character of an animal, which makes it special and unique

predators   animals that depend on other, usually smaller or slower, animals for food

pus   a yellow or green liquid that oozes out of infected cuts

rodents   animals with strong front teeth for gnawing

rosettes   rounded twirling shapes

saline solution   salt dissolved in water

shelter   place where abandoned pets are cared for until they find a new home

sores   open places on the skin, usually infected with germs

sow   a female guinea pig

stress   tension caused by feeling bad or worried in body or mind

symptom   a small thing that tells you what the bigger problem might be

territory   place an animal lives and marks as its own

urinate   to wee

urine   wee, liquid passed out of the body containing water and waste

vitamin C   vitamin found in plants that keeps animals healthy

vomit   to be sick

worms   parasites that live in other animals

zoonoses   diseases that are passed between animals and people

Further reading

Care for Your Guinea Pig (*RSPCA Pet Guides* Series), Steve Cheetham (Foreword) (Collins, 2004)

Guinea Pig: An Owner's Guide to a Happy Healthy Pet (*Happy Healthy Pet* Series), Audrey Pavia (Hungry Minds Inc, 2005)

Guinea Pigs (Collins Family Pet Guides), Peter Gurney (Collins, 1999)

The Wild Side of Pet Guinea Pigs (*The Wild Side of Pets* Series), Jo Waters (Raintree, 2004)

Useful addresses

Most countries have organizations and societies that work to protect animals from cruelty and to help people learn how to care for the pets they live with properly.

UK
Royal Society for the Prevention of
    Cruelty to Animals (RSPCA)
Wilberforce Way
Southwater
Horsham
West Sussex
RH13 9RS
Tel: 0870 33 35 999
Fax: 0870 75 30 284

Australia
RSPCA Australia Inc
PO Box 265
Deakin West ACT 2600
Australia
Tel: 02 6282 8300
Fax: 02 6282 8311

Internet

UK
RSPCA
www.rspca.org.uk

Good information and online shop
www.petplanet.co.uk/petplanet/kids/
    kidsguineapig.htm

Australia
www.rspca.org.au

Disclaimer
All the Internet addresses (URLs) given in this book were valid at the time of going to press. However, due to the dynamic nature of the Internet, some addresses may have changed, or sites may have changed or ceased to exist since publication. While the author and Publishers regret any inconvenience this may cause readers, no responsibility for any such changes can be accepted by either the author or the Publishers.

Index